Your Angel

by Becky De Oliveira

Illustrated by Alice De Marco

'Angel,' the boy said, 'I need you to pay attention.
I'm going to ride my bicycle with no hands.
I want to ride all the way to the end of the street.
You need to be ready to catch me if I fall.
OK? Here I go.'

Before he was halfway to the end of the street, the boy's bicycle hit a hump. The front wheel twisted and he fell. He grazed his elbow and it bled and stung. The boy sat on the ground and sobbed. 'Angel,' he said, 'why didn't you catch me? You're not a very good angel.'

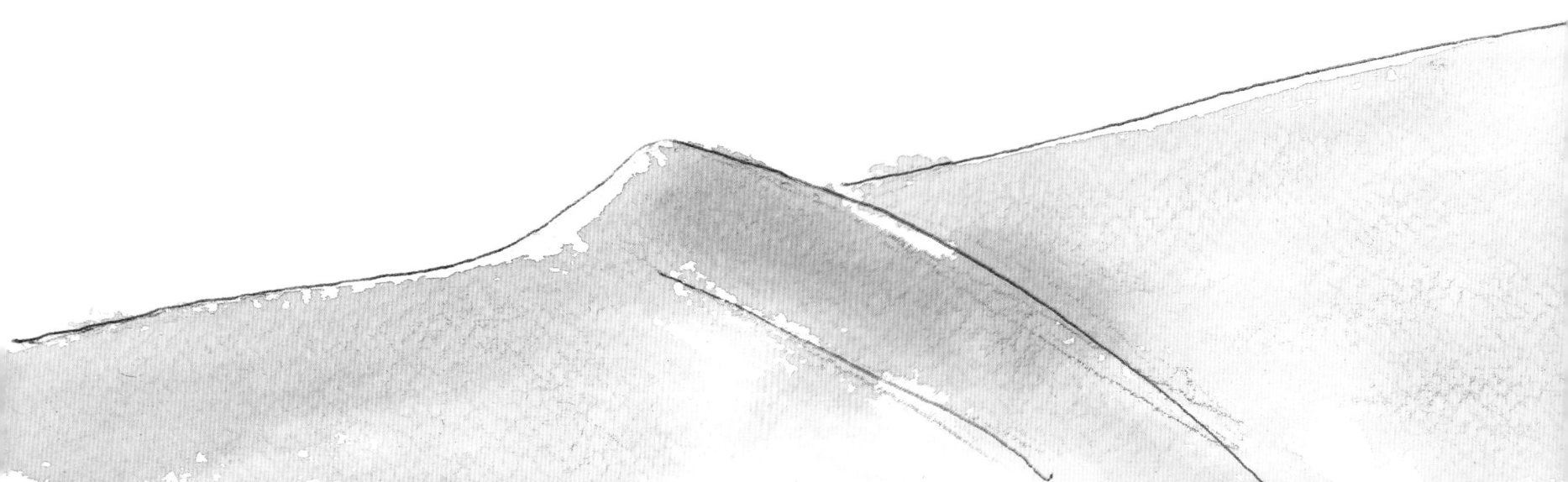

After supper the boy took a bath. 'Angel,' he said, 'I'm going to float on my back. I need you to keep my head from going under. Are you ready? Here I go.'

The boy's head dipped just under the water and it went in his nose and stung his eyes. He sat up, coughing and spitting and wiping his face with his hands.
'Angel,' he said, 'you're a bad angel.'

After his mother had read his bedtime story and he'd brushed his teeth and said his prayers, the boy lay in bed and stared at the ceiling. It was covered with stars and moons that glowed in the dark. The boy thought for a long time. Then he said in a soft voice, 'Angel, I want to see you. Can you show me what you look like?'

Nothing happened.

The boy spoke louder. 'Angel,' he said, 'this is your last chance. You haven't done anything I've asked today. If you don't show me what you look like, then I'm not your friend anymore.'

Nothing.

'I'm going to count to three,' the boy said. 'I'm going to close my eyes and when I say "three" I'm going to open them and you will be standing by my bed, shining and bright. And if you're not, then I don't like you anymore. OK? Here I go.'

'ONE,' the boy said, squeezing his eyes shut tight.

'TWO . . .

'THREE!' He shouted the three in such a loud voice that at the very moment he opened his eyes the lights came on and Mummy was standing in the door with her arms folded across her chest.

'Why are you shouting?' she asked.

'Tell me the truth,' the boy said. 'The whole truth. Is there really such a thing as a guardian angel?'

'I believe there is,' Mummy answered.

The boy started to cry. 'I can't see my angel and he won't show me what he looks like. He didn't catch me when I fell off my bike and he didn't help me float in the bathtub. He doesn't help me do anything. Do you think if I ask God I can get a better angel?'

Mummy smiled. 'I don't know,' she said. 'Why don't we try?'

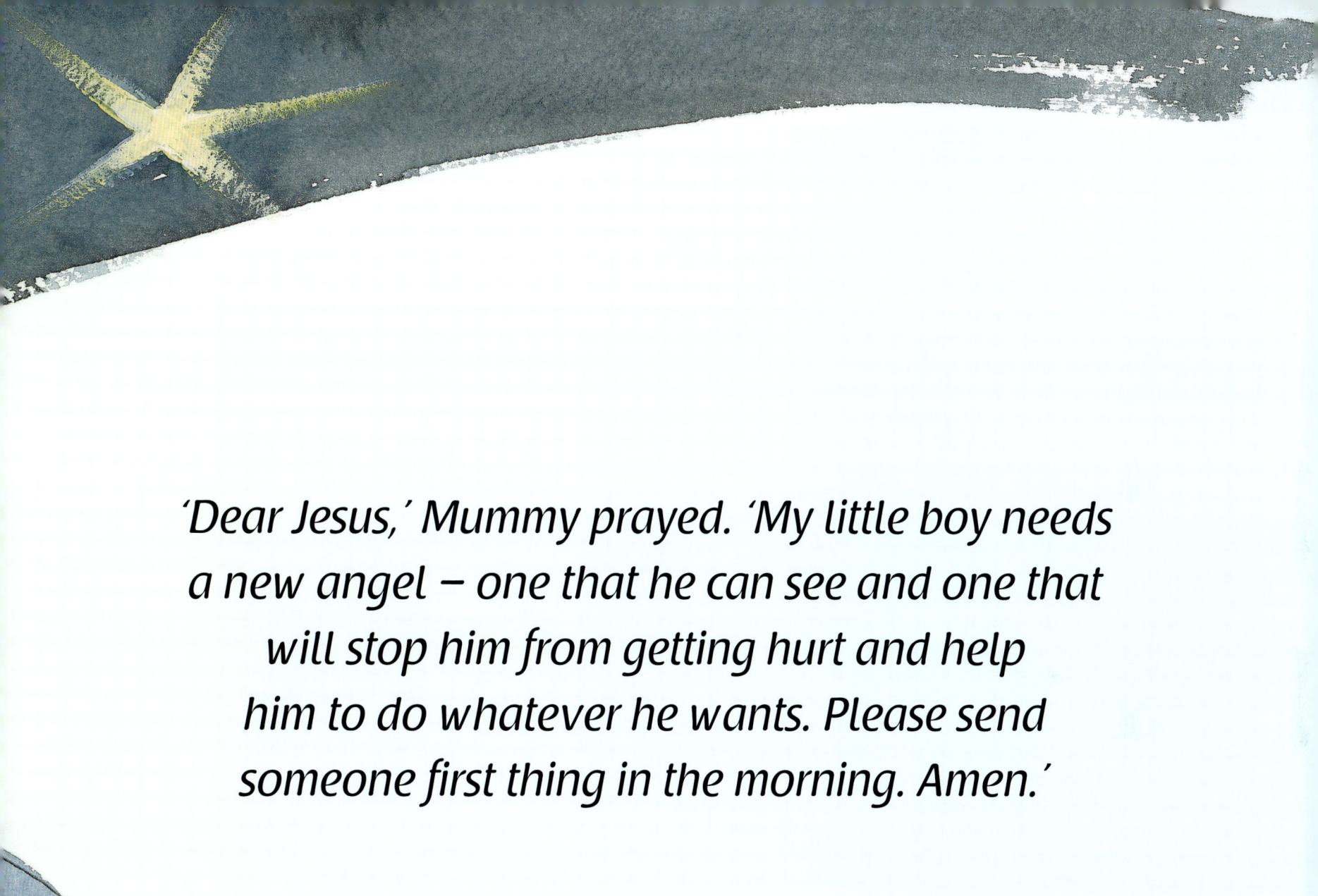

'Dear Jesus,' Mummy prayed. 'My little boy needs a new angel – one that he can see and one that will stop him from getting hurt and help him to do whatever he wants. Please send someone first thing in the morning. Amen.'

'Do you think it will work?' the boy asked.

'We'll see,' Mummy said. She kissed him on the forehead.
'Goodnight, Bugaboo.'

The next morning, Mummy wore a long white dress.
At breakfast, she stood behind the boy with
her arms outstretched, almost touching him.
'What are you doing?' the boy asked.

'I am your angel for the day,' Mummy said. 'You can see me, can't you? Right now, I am making sure you don't choke on your food. I'm ready, you see, to slap you on the back if you start to cough.'

The boy frowned.

'No, no,' Mummy said. 'Wait! It gets better.
I'm going to ride with you to school today
and sit next to you on the bus.
No one will dare make faces at you
with me sitting there.

'And if you forget one of your spelling words,
I will whisper the answer in your ear.
At break-time, I'll hold your legs while you swing
on the big iron rings, and that way you're
sure not to fall. We can go down the big
slide together, you and I. You will sit on
my lap and I won't let you go too fast.'

The boy frowned.

'Wait,' Mummy said, 'it gets better. When we come home, I'll follow you on your bicycle and make sure you don't crash. No. Better still, I'll ride the bike and you can sit on the bar in front of me. And when you take your bath, I will hold on to your arms the whole time to make sure you don't slip.'

Mummy beamed. 'It's going to be a perfect day,' she said. 'You will be so happy.'

'I don't know,' the boy said, still frowning. 'It doesn't sound like fun.'

'Ah,' Mummy said. 'I think I know how you feel. God knows how you feel, too. You want to be free. Your life wouldn't be any fun if there were someone tagging along, getting in your way, doing everything for you. That's why you can't see your angel. That's why your angel doesn't always stop you from getting hurt or help you do all the things you want to do. You have to do things yourself. Sometimes you have to fall. That's how you learn.

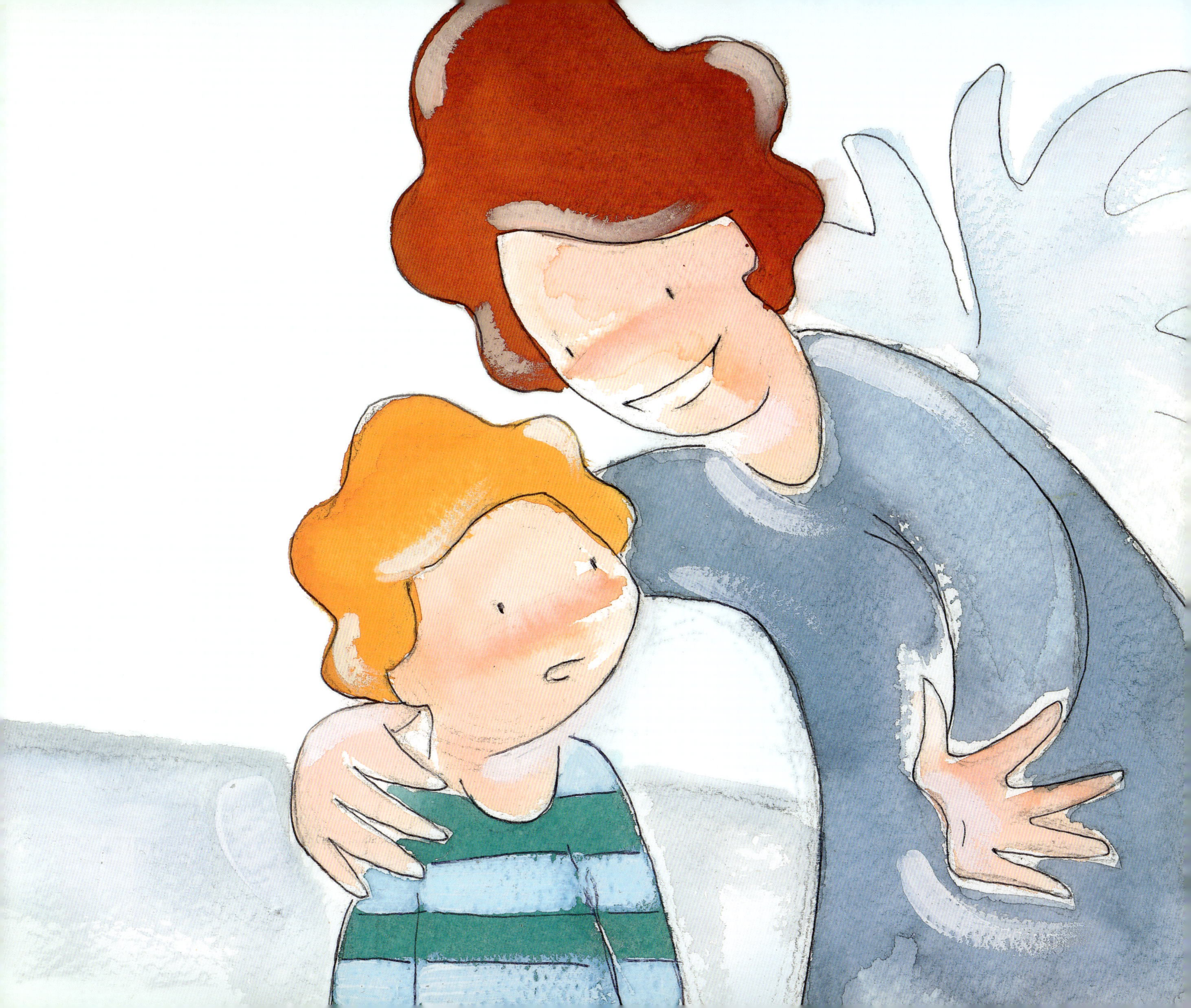

'Your angel is everywhere,' Mummy said. 'When you fall and graze your knee, at first it hurts, but then there's that moment where the pain starts to lift. That's your angel kissing your knee with his cool lips.

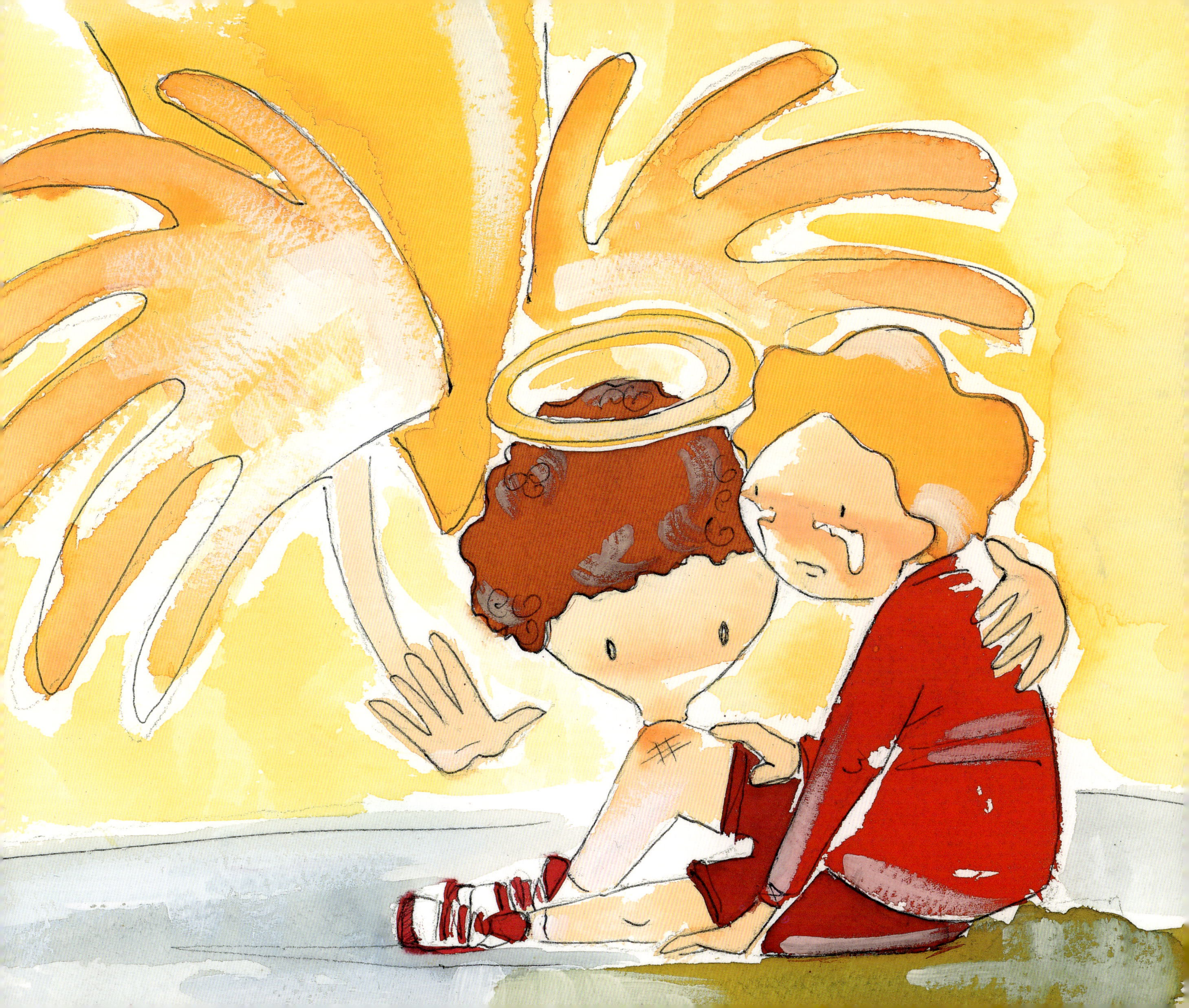

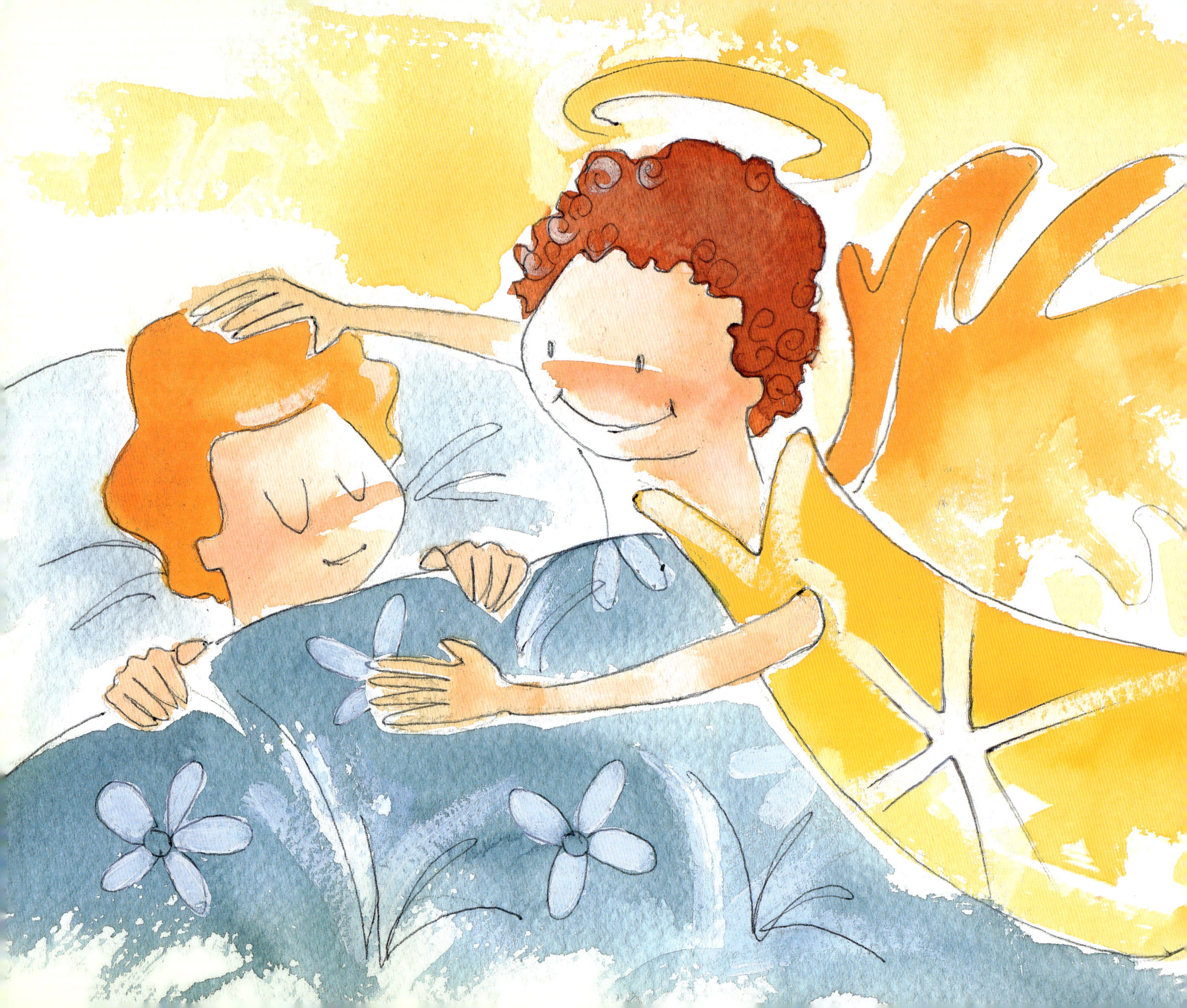

'When you're lying in bed afraid of the dark and you can't go to sleep, but finally your eyes grow heavy and you begin to nod off, that's your angel stroking your hair.

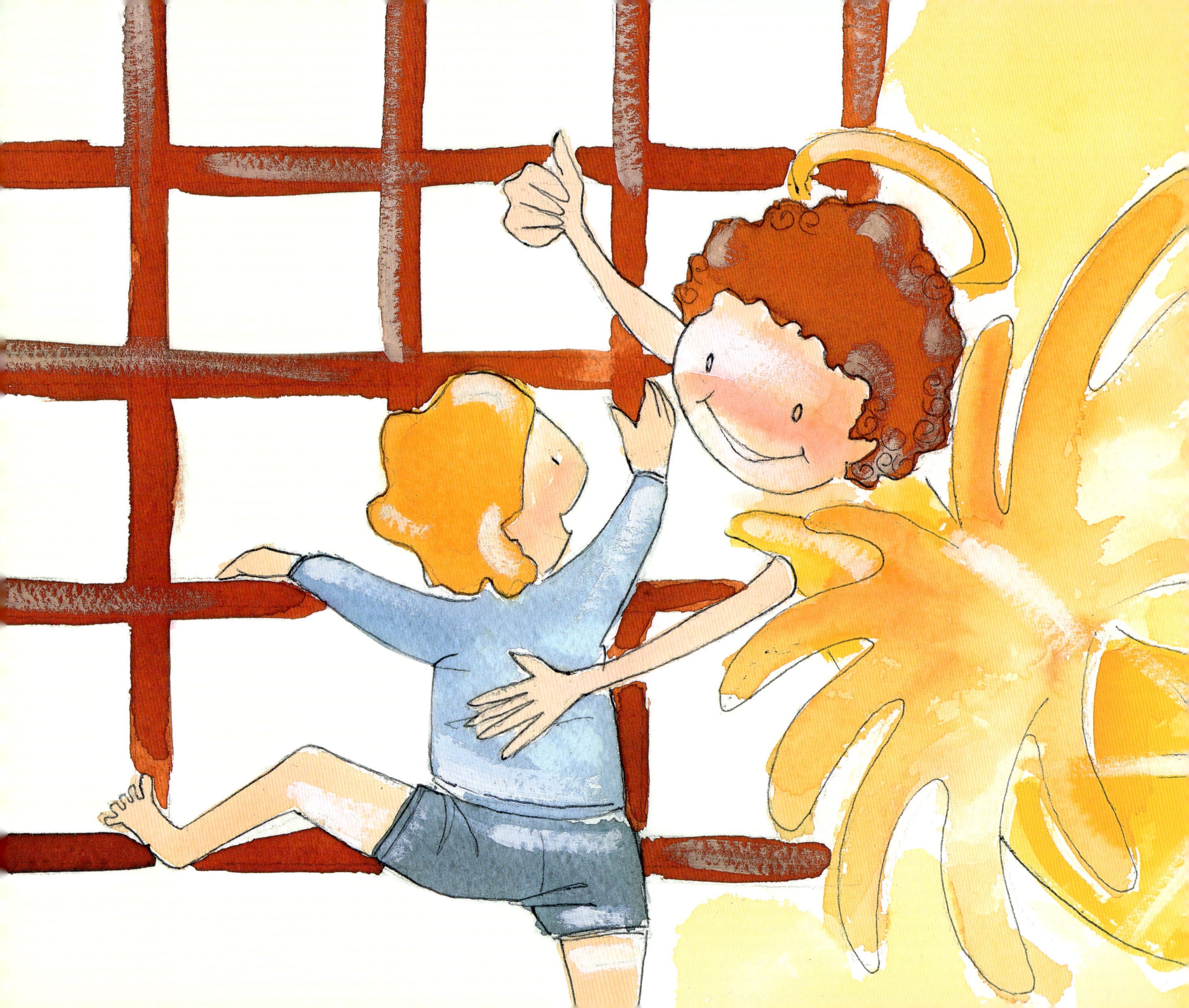

'When you fall from the
climbing frame at school
and yet you get back
up and try again,
that's your angel,
lifting you to your feet.

'When you stand on the high diving board at the swimming pool and you're too afraid to jump, your angel is there whispering, "You can do this."

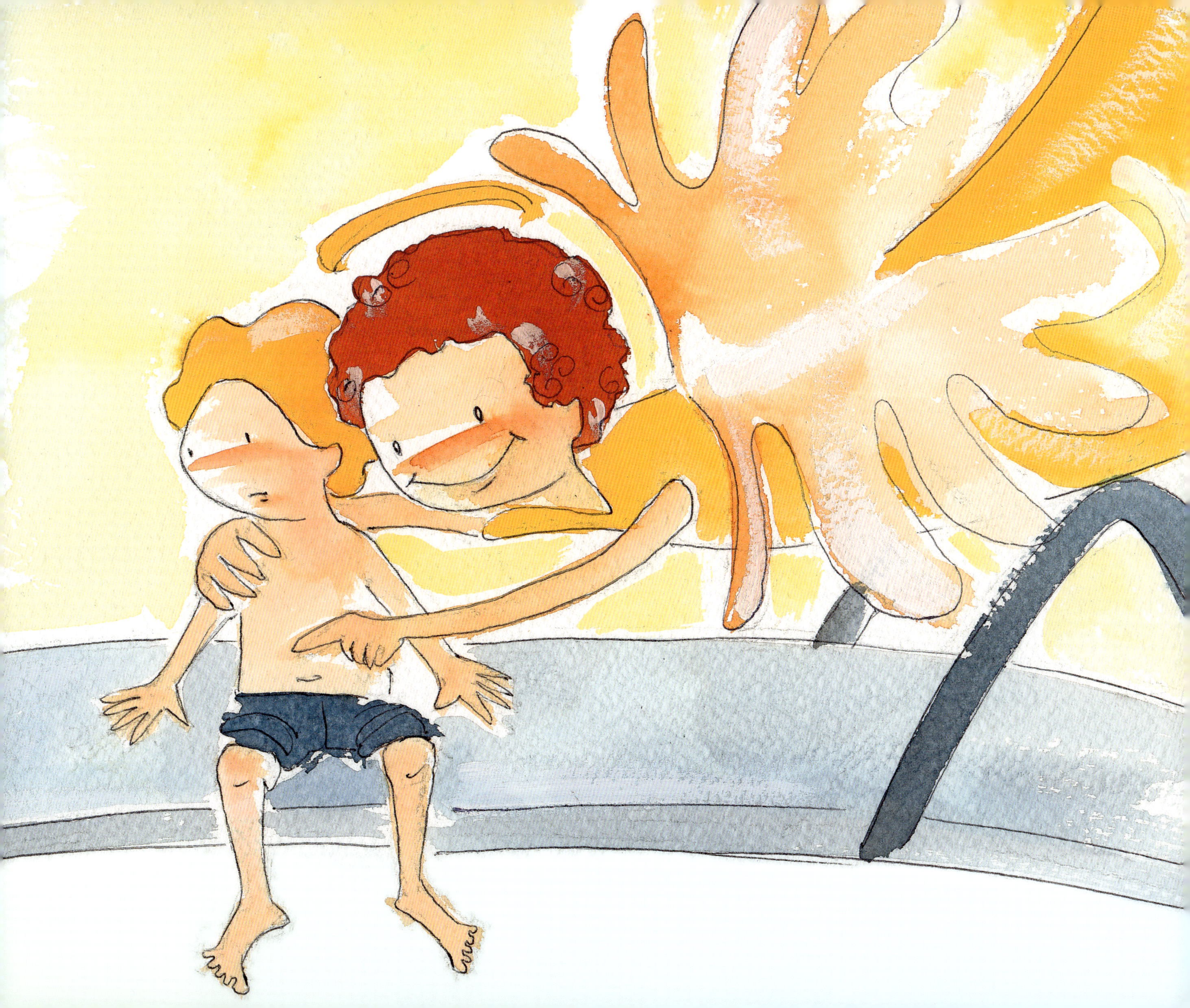

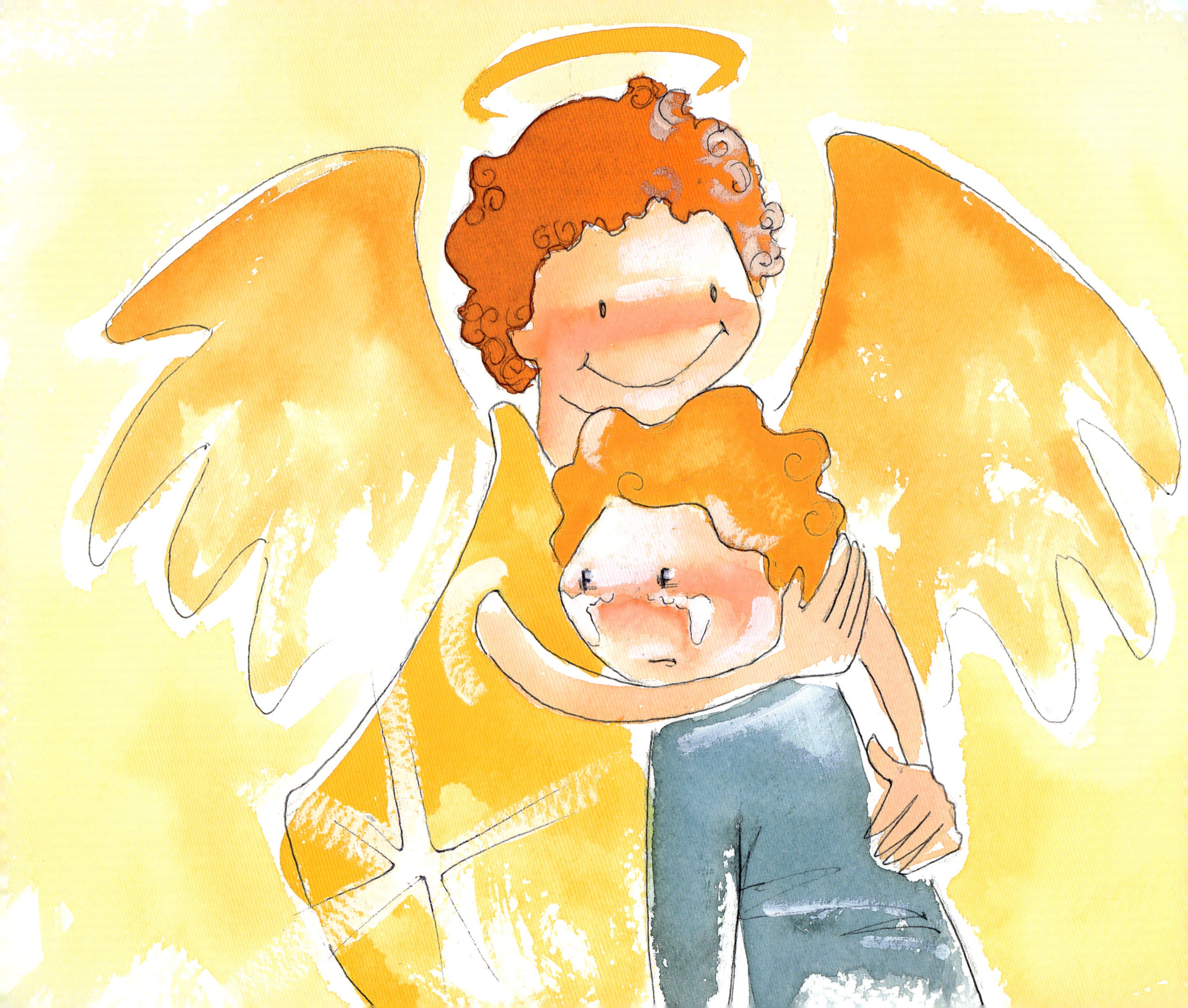

'When people say mean things
to you that hurt your feelings, your angel
puts his arms around you and gives
you a squeeze to remind you that
God loves you forever.'

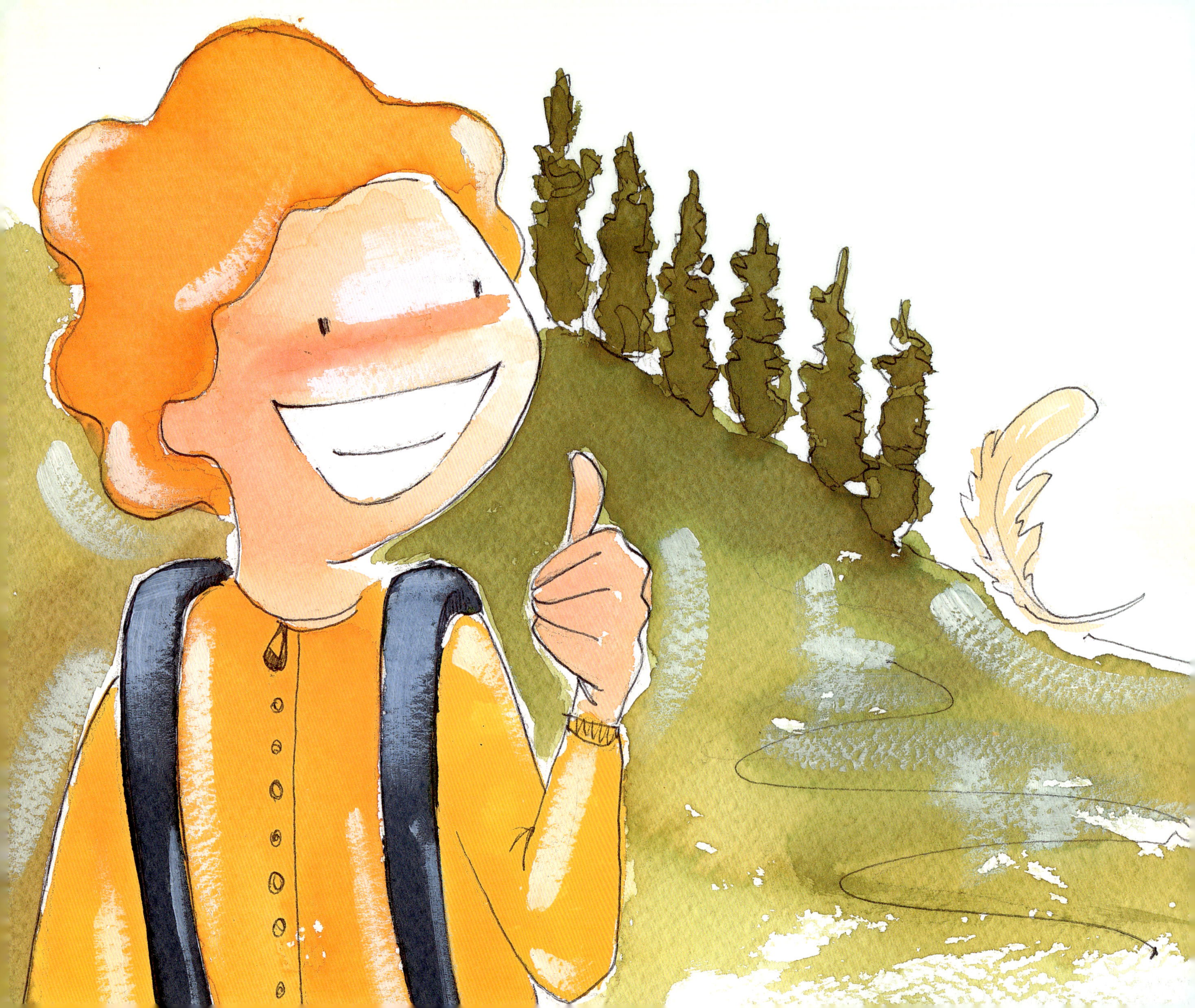

The boy started down the hill to
catch the bus to school.
Suddenly he smiled to himself.
'Angel,' he said, 'I'm going to run
down this hill as fast as my legs will go.
You'll see only a streak of yellow that's my jacket.
Cheer for me, Angel! Clap your hands!'

And the boy ran.

First published in 2009
Copyright © 2009 Autumn House Publishing (Europe) Ltd.

Author: Becky De Oliveira
Illustrator: Alice De Marco

All rights reserved. No part of this publication
may be reproduced in any form without
prior permission from the publisher.
British Library Cataloguing in Publication Data.
A catalogue record for this book is
available from the British Library.

ISBN 978-1-906381-67-7

Published by
Autumn House,
Alma Park, Grantham, Lincs.

Printed in Thailand